13 most i BIBLE Lessons

for kids about

LOVING EACH OTHER

Group
Real. **Bold.** Love.

Loveland, Colorado
group.com

Copyright © 2014 Group Publishing, Inc

Visit our website: group.com

Forms mentioned in this book are available at group.com/reproducibles

CREDITS
Contributing Authors: Anne Bosarge, Danielle Christy, Siv Ricketts, Larry Shallenberger, Emily Snider, Amy Weaver, Vicki L.O. Witte, Henry Zonio
Executive Editor: Christine Yount Jones
Managing Editors: Jennifer Hooks, Adam Mackie
Associate Editor: David Jennings
Assistant Editor: Becky Helzer
Cover Design: Rebecca Swain
Book Design: Jean Bruns
Production: Kate Elvin

Unless otherwise indicated, all Scripture quotations are taken from the *Holy Bible* New Living Translation, copyright © 1996, 2004, 2007, 2013. Used by permission of Tyndale House Publishers, Inc., Carol Stream, Illinois 60188. All rights reserved.

ISBN 978-1-4707-1523-6

6 5 4 3 2 1   19 16 17 16 15 14

Printed in the United States of America.

CONTENTS

INTRODUCTION

Ask people who minister to children what they want most, and you'll hear something like this:

"I want kids to know the Bible."

"I want children to have a strong relationship with God."

"I want kids to have a faith foundation that'll stand the test of time."

That's what the *13 Most Important Bible Lessons for Kids* series is all about—helping kids build a strong foundation in the basics of their faith. In *13 Most Important Bible Lessons for Kids About Loving Each Other,* you'll draw children closer to Jesus and help them learn through his example and those who followed him how to show others God's love. Each lesson uses Scripture, conversation, and hands-on experiences to teach kids vital truths that include:

We love each other as God loves us. (1 Peter 1:22)

We love each other. (John 13:35)

We forgive each other. (Ephesians 4:32)

We serve each other. (John 13:14)

We don't cause each other to sin. (Galatians 5:13)

We're humble toward each other. (Luke 14:7-14)

We live in harmony with each other. (Romans 12:16)

We accept each other. (Romans 15:7)

We don't judge each other. (Matthew 7:1-5)

We're united with each other. (1 Corinthians 1:10-17)

We bear each other's burdens. (Galatians 6:1-3)

We pray for each other. (James 5:13-18)

We encourage each other. (Hebrews 3:7-13)

These lessons won't fill your kids with theoretical information they'll soon forget. Instead, we've designed the lessons to transform your kids by engaging them in learning experiences that'll help them know the loving God who created them and sustains them.

7

Here's the flow for each lesson:

Set the Foundation—Engages kids in an opening activity to get them enthused and wanting more.

Present the Bible Foundation—This is the "meat" of the lesson, designed to help kids dig into the Bible.

Build on the Foundation—Once kids have discovered a way God wants us to love others, they respond and apply what they've learned in a meaningful way—then pray.

Jesus told a much-loved parable about the need to build a strong faith foundation. You know the parable: The wise man built his house upon the rock...and nothing could tear down that house! *In 13 Most Important Bible Lessons for Kids About Loving Each Other,* you can build conversations with children upon strong biblical foundations.

This is what you dream of, plan for, and pray about in ministry—that the children you minister to will have such a strong faith foundation that nothing will be able to tear down their faith. May God use *13 Most Important Bible Lessons for Kids About Loving Each Other* as you lead children in loving God and loving others.

Be aware that some children have food allergies that can be dangerous. Know your children, and consult with parents about allergies their children may have. Also be sure to read food labels carefully as hidden ingredients can cause allergy-related problems.

To avoid choking hazards, be sure to pick up pieces of any broken balloons promptly. Balloons may contain latex.

LESSON **1**

We Love Each Other as God Loves Us

God's love is infinite. Unconditional. Limitless. He's the very definition of love. He showed the depth of his love by sending his Son as a sacrifice for our sins—the very thing that separated us from him. Is it possible for us to love others in the same way? It can be challenging to show love to those who frustrate us, hurt us, or are different from us.

The truth is, it's impossible to show that kind of love to others through our own efforts. The only way to love others the way God loves us is through the power of the Holy Spirit. When we love God with all our heart, his love shines through us and touches others. As you teach kids about loving others, encourage them by continually pointing back to the One who loved us first.

Scripture Foundation

1 PETER 1:22
God wants us to love each other as brothers and sisters.

1 JOHN 4:8-12
God loves us so we can love others.

JOHN 13:34
Jesus tells us to love others as he loved us.

THIS LESSON AT A GLANCE

SEQUENCE	EXPERIENCES	SUPPLIES
SET THE FOUNDATION (about 10 minutes)	**On One Condition** Kids will discover more about God's unconditional love by earning a prize for their efforts.	• small toys or trinkets (such as stickers or pencil toppers), 2 per preteen
PRESENT THE BIBLE FOUNDATION (about 25 minutes)	**Do the Math** Kids will use their own words to dig into the Bible, play a tasting game, and create math equations about God's love.	• kid-friendly Bibles (preferably NLT) • paper • pens • bowl of jelly beans in assorted colors • poster board • marker
BUILD ON THE FOUNDATION (about 10 minutes)	**Filled With Love** Kids will compare a deflated and inflated balloon with what's it like to be filled with God's love.	• uninflated balloons, 1 per preteen • slips of paper, 1 per preteen • pens

On One Condition

(about 10 minutes)

Welcome kids, and announce that you've brought a special treat.

Have kids form two lines. Alternating between lines, ask kids to step forward one at a time to get a treat. Randomly ask some of the kids to do something to get the treat, such as sing a song or do jumping jacks. Other times, just give the treat freely. Be sure not to do the same thing for each line; change it up so kids don't know what to expect.

After everyone has had a turn, have kids sit down.

ASK:
- **What was this experience like for you?**
- **What was it like when you had to work for your treat?**
- **What are some things people do to make their friends work for the treat of their friendship—instead of just giving friendship?**

SAY:
It might seem strange to set up conditions for friendship, but we sometimes do this to one another. I have another toy to share. This time, though, you don't have to do anything at all to get it.

Give each person a small toy.

ASK:
- **Explain why you think we sometimes put conditions on giving our love or friendship.**
- **Describe the conditions, if any, you think God puts on his love for us.**

SAY:
Today we're going to discover what the Bible says about God's unconditional love.

11

Do the Math

(about 25 minutes)

Have kids form pairs, and give each pair a sheet of paper, a pen, and a Bible. Then read aloud 1 Peter 1:22.

See page 8.

SAY:

We're going to do a quick Bible study. I'm going to give each pair a different word from this verse. Partners will work together to come up with synonyms—words that mean the same thing as the word I give you. You'll have two minutes to write as many words as you can come up with.

Give each pair one of these words (it's okay for multiple pairs to have the same word): *cleansed, sins, obeyed, sincere, love, deeply.*

After two minutes, call kids together. Ask each pair to tell how many words they came up with. Congratulate everyone for their work.

Once again, read aloud 1 Peter 1:22 below and pause where indicated to let kids fill in their synonyms.

"You were cleansed (pause) **from your sins** (pause) **when you obeyed** (pause) **the truth, so now you must show sincere** (pause) **love to each other as brothers and sisters. Love** (pause) **each other deeply** (pause) **with all your heart."**

ASK:
- **What did the words you came up with teach you about what this verse means?**
- **What did our Bible study tell you about how God wants us to love one another?**
- **Tell about a time you felt this sincere kind of love from someone.**

SAY:

The Bible tells us to love each other; and sometimes that might seem like a challenge.

Set out the bowl of jelly beans. Have kids call out their favorite color of jelly bean and form groups with kids who share a favorite color. Then give each person any jelly bean other than their favorite color, and ask them to eat it. As kids eat, have them share about a time it was hard for them to love someone (without naming names).

ASK:
- **What did you think when you got stuck with a jelly bean you didn't especially like?**
- **What have you done when you've gotten stuck spending time with a person you don't like?**

SAY:
Giving sincere love to one another can be challenging. But it's something God expects us to do. In fact, God has shown us what true love adds up to.

Read aloud 1 John 4:8, and then write this equation for God's love on a piece of poster board: Anyone - love = someone - God.

SAY:
Let's see if we can do the math again about God's love for verse 9.

Read aloud 1 John 4:9, and then write on the poster board God + love + Jesus = eternal life.

Now challenge kids to "do the math" as you read 1 John 4:10-12 one verse at a time and then write down suggested ideas on the poster board. It's okay if kids come up with different things. Dive in to help if necessary with ideas from the "It All Adds Up" box near the end of this lesson segment.

ASK:
- **What did you learn about God's love from this Bible study?**
- **What does this mean: "Anyone who does not love does not know God"?**
- **How do these verses make you want to add God's love for others to your life?**

SAY:
It can be challenging to love others unconditionally, especially when they hurt us or make us mad. But even though we sin and do wrong things, God sent his Son, Jesus, to die on the cross as a sacrifice to pay the price for our sins. We didn't deserve that kind of love from God, and

13

we can't earn it. It's unconditional. God did it simply because he loves us. When we love God with all our heart, he helps us show that same love to others. **And Jesus says...**Read aloud John 13:34.

IT ALL ADDS UP

Verse 10: Real love = God sending Jesus to - our sins
Verse 11: God + love = us + love for others
Verse 12: 0 = anyone who's seen God.
When we love each other = infinity

BUILD ON THE FOUNDATION

Filled With Love

(about 10 minutes)

Show kids a deflated balloon.

BALLOON WARNING

See page 8.

ASK:
- **What stopped this balloon from fulfilling its purpose?**
- **What stops you from loving others the way God wants you to?**

SAY:
A deflated balloon doesn't do much or serve its purpose very well. Our hearts are the same way. When we don't fill ourselves with God's love, we're empty and aren't able to love others the way God wants us to.

14

ASK:
- **What are ways we can fill our hearts with God's love?**

As kids offer answers, inflate the balloon. Explain to kids that this is like what happens to our hearts when we accept God's unconditional love and love others the same way.

Give everyone a slip of paper, a pen, and an uninflated balloon. On the slips of paper, have kids each write one way they can show God's love to someone this week. When everyone is done, have kids each roll up their slip of paper and put it inside their balloon. Have kids inflate and tie off the balloons.

PRAY:

Dear God, thank you so much for loving us. You know everything about us—when we do right and when we do wrong—and you still love us unconditionally. Help us follow your example and love others as you love us. In Jesus' name, amen.

Have kids toss their balloons in the air and let them fall to the ground. Then have kids each pick up the balloon closest to them. Encourage them to take the balloon home, pop it, and complete the action on the slip inside for someone this week.

LESSON 2
We Love Each Other

Our world teaches preteens that seeing is believing. And while we may not be able to see God, it's through the loving actions and grace of his followers that others can experience and understand God's love. Not everyone saw Jesus when he was on earth, yet his early followers successfully spread his love and message to the world—through love. Many people today may have heard of Jesus the man, but they haven't experienced his life-changing love. In this lesson, your preteens will learn that God wants us to show the world who Jesus is through our love for one another.

Scripture Foundation

JOHN 13:35
Our love for one another is proof that we're Jesus' disciples.

1 JOHN 4:12
God's love is brought to full expression in us.

ACTS 2:42-47
The early church loved God and one another.

MATTHEW 5:43-47
Jesus commands us to love everyone.

THIS LESSON AT A GLANCE

SEQUENCE	EXPERIENCES	SUPPLIES	
SET THE FOUNDATION (about 10 minutes)	***Looking for Proof*** Kids will learn about showing and spreading God's love.	• kid-friendly Bible (preferably NLT) • 4 clear glass drinking cups • baby powder • clear tape • 4 small paintbrushes	• black construction paper • 4 washable ink pads • white paper • pens • wet wipes
PRESENT THE BIBLE FOUNDATION (about 25 minutes)	***The Evidence*** Kids will act out ways the early church showed love to others.	• kid-friendly Bibles (preferably NLT) • 4 shoe boxes • a few coins, a piece of cloth, a few small stones, a scroll	• paper • pens or pencils • 1 copy of the "Suspect Profiles" handout (at the end of this lesson) • scissors
BUILD ON THE FOUNDATION (about 10 minutes)	***Leaving Our Mark*** Kids will decide on one way they can show God's love.	• 4 washable ink pads • wet wipes • card stock • fine-tipped markers • several pairs of scissors	

Before the Lesson

SET THE FOUNDATION: *LOOKING FOR PROOF*—Secretly have four kids each touch the outside of one of four drinking cups so that each cup is covered with the fingerprints of only one preteen. Instruct the kids to not reveal their identities during the experience.

PRESENT THE BIBLE FOUNDATION: *THE EVIDENCE*—Print a copy of the "Suspect Profiles" handout (at the end of this lesson and available at group.com/reproducibles), and cut apart the pieces. Place one profile in each shoe box along with the corresponding item:

- **Barnabas: Acts 4:32-37 (coins)**
- **Tabitha: Acts 9:36-43 (piece of cloth)**
- **Stephen: Acts 7:54-69 (small stones)**
- **Priscilla and Aquila: Acts 18:24-28 (a scroll)**

Looking for Proof

(about 10 minutes)

Welcome kids, and have them form four groups. Ensure each group contains one of the kids who touched a drinking cup beforehand, and have each group sit in a circle.

SAY:
I have a mystery, and I need super-sleuths to solve it! Someone's been using my drinking cups, and I think it's someone in this room.

ASK:
• How do you think we can solve this mystery?

Explain to kids that they can help you solve the mystery by dusting for fingerprints, and you'll begin by making a record of everyone's fingerprints.

Distribute ink pads, pens, and sheets of white paper to each group. Have each pre-teen press one thumb on an ink pad and then make a thumbprint on a sheet of paper. Then ask kids to write their name next to their print and use a wet wipe to clean the ink off their fingers.

SAY:
Now we're going to take turns dusting the cups for matching fingerprints.

Give each group a small paintbrush and a sheet of black construction paper. Distribute the drinking cups (holding them carefully so as not to disturb the fingerprints) so each group has the cup one of their members touched. Have groups take turns sprinkling a small amount of powder onto the outside of each glass. (Placing a sheet of paper under the glass will catch excess powder.) Let kids take turns using the paintbrush to gently brush away excess powder, exposing fingerprints. Show kids how to place a piece of clear tape on top of a print and then lift the tape and place it on a piece of black construction paper to reveal the white outline of a fingerprint. Continue this process until all preteens have had a turn dusting for and gathering fingerprints.

19

SAY:
Now that we have the proof, carefully compare the fingerprints you lifted with the fingerprint records we made.

Give kids two minutes to compare fingerprints and guess who held the cups. Tell kids whether they guessed correctly.

ASK:

- **Describe how easy or difficult it was to solve this mystery, and why.**
- **How were you able to prove who'd actually held the cups?**

Read aloud John 13:35 and 1 John 4:12.

SAY:

That connection between your fingerprints and you is a lot like the connection between the evidence of God's love and God. None of us has ever seen God, but the Bible tells us that people who follow God show love to others so the world can see who Jesus is.

ASK:

- **Tell about a time someone showed you God's love.**
- **How are people who follow God like God's fingerprints in the world?**

SAY:

Jesus tells us to love others—even our enemies—by following his example. When we won't love others, we aren't showing the world who Jesus is. It's not always easy to love others all the time, but that's what Jesus tells us to do. Let's look at some people in the Bible who helped show the world who Jesus is.

PRESENT THE BIBLE FOUNDATION

The Evidence

(about 25 minutes)

Have kids remain in their groups, and show them the four shoe boxes.

SAY:

You're great detectives! Now I need your help with something else. Inside each of these boxes is a suspect profile and a piece of evidence. Each suspect is guilty of spreading God's love and showing others who Jesus is. Your group's mission is to study the profile and present the case to the bigger group. You must use the piece of evidence in your portrayal.

Give each group a shoe box. Allow about eight minutes for kids to read the suspect profiles and practice their presentations. When time's up, have everyone form a circle.

SAY:

Each group is going to take turns describing or acting out its case. Then we'll compare how each of our suspects showed love and how we can follow that example today.

Let kids in each group take a turn, using the evidence in the box as they describe their case. After each group has finished, discuss the following questions with the larger group.

ASK:

• How did the person(s) show God's love?
• How can we follow that example today?

SAY:

Great job presenting your suspects and displaying the evidence! One other thing these suspects have in common is that they were part of the early church—the first group of people who followed Jesus.

Give each person a sheet of paper and a pen or pencil.

SAY:

Let's see how people in the early church showed their love for one another, and compare it with what we do today. After each verse I read, you'll have 30 seconds to silently draw what that love looks like for people who follow Jesus today.

Read aloud Acts 2:42, and then pause.
Read aloud Acts 2:43, and then pause.
Read aloud Acts 2:44, and then pause.
Read aloud Acts 2:45, and then pause.
Read aloud Acts 2:46-47, and then pause.

21

LESSON 2: We Love Each Other

SAY:

The world knew who Jesus' followers were because of their love—not just for each other but also to strangers and even their enemies.

Have kids open their Bibles, and ask for a willing preteen to read aloud Matthew 5:43-47.

ASK:
- Why is loving others sometimes difficult?
- Tell about a time it was difficult for you to love someone, and why.
- What are ways we can remember to love others so they see Jesus' through us—even when it's challenging?

SAY:

Loving others isn't always easy, but we can do it with God's help! Now we're going to work on a top-secret project to share love with others.

BUILD ON THE FOUNDATION

Leaving Our Mark

(about 10 minutes)

Distribute card stock and scissors, and have available ink pads, markers, and wet wipes. Have kids each cut out a 1-inch paper square.

SAY:

We learned earlier that we're like God's fingerprints, spreading his love around the world so people know who Jesus is. Today we're going to spread God's love to those who really need it—super-sleuth style.

Have kids silently think of one person they struggle to show love to or someone they know who needs love.

22

SAY:

As you think of this person, make a thumb-print heart on your paper square.

Show kids how to make a thumbprint heart by pressing a thumb on the ink pad and overlapping two prints in a V-shape to create a heart shape on the paper. As kids work, ask them to think about one way they can show love to that person—without the person knowing. On the back of the paper, have kids write in small letters "God's fingerprints are on you." Have kids clean their hands with wet wipes.

Tell kids that after they've secretly done the act of love, they can leave their thumbprint heart behind where the person will find it as a mystery clue.

SAY:

We can't see God. But just like our fingerprints leave marks everywhere we touch, our love leaves a mark on the hearts of those it touches and shows them who Jesus is.

Have kids bow their heads, and let them know there'll be a time for them to silently pray for the people they thought of who need love.

PRAY:

Dear God, help us be your fingerprints in this world, spreading your love to everyone we meet. Help us love not only our friends and family, but even our enemies. Help us love these people (have kids pray silently for the people they thought of). **Help us, through our love, show the world who Jesus is. In Jesus' name, amen.**

Suspect Profiles

Barnabas: Acts 4:32-37

Tabitha: Acts 9:36-43

Stephen: Acts 7:54-69

Priscilla and Aquila: Acts 18:24-28

13 MOST IMPORTANT BIBLE LESSONS FOR KIDS ABOUT LOVING EACH OTHER

LESSON 3
We Forgive Each Other

Forgiveness is difficult work; this is true whether you're a CEO or a preteen. Letting go of the hurt and anger we feel when someone wounds us is challenging. And forgiveness is uniquely difficult for preteens, since it's during this stage when they develop fierce loyalties to friends and they're testing newly discovered (and still awkward) social skills. Preteens try on and discard ways of relating like clothing in a mall dressing room. Inevitably, one friend will offend another and the end result is hurt and confusion. The upside is this dynamic creates ever-present opportunities for kids to practice forgiveness.

Preteens are also characterized by black-and-white thinking and a keen sense of justice. When preteens feel a situation is wrong or unfair, they're quick to grow indignant. This lesson is designed to remind preteens that even when they've been wounded or hurt, God urges them to take the next step. They can forgive when they've been wronged because they've been forgiven by God, who's been wronged infinitely more.

Scripture Foundation

EPHESIANS 4:32
We forgive others because God forgave us.

MATTHEW 18:21-35
There's no end to how much forgiveness we give.

HEBREWS 12:15
Protect yourself against bitterness that grows up to trouble you.

PROVERBS 17:9
Friendships suffer when we refuse to forgive.

THIS LESSON AT A GLANCE

SEQUENCE	EXPERIENCES	SUPPLIES
SET THE FOUNDATION (about 10 minutes)	***Tough-O-Meters*** Kids will measure how hard or easy it would be to forgive people in a variety of situations.	• kid-friendly Bible (preferably NLT) • pads of sticky notes
PRESENT THE BIBLE FOUNDATION (about 25 minutes)	***Text a Parable*** Kids will create a series of text messages that recount the parable of the unforgiving debtor from the perspective of each person involved.	• kid-friendly Bibles (preferably NLT) • markers • neon poster board • scissors • 1 copy of the "Dialogue Bubble Template" handout (at the end of this lesson)
BUILD ON THE FOUNDATION (about 10 minutes)	***The Price of Forgiveness*** Kids will explore Matthew 18:21-22 and compare the offenses others have committed against them with how much God has forgiven them.	• kid-friendly Bibles (preferably NLT) • tissue paper • pens • bowl of water

Before the Lesson

PRESENT THE BIBLE FOUNDATION: *TEXT A PARABLE*— Print a copy of the "Dialogue Bubble Template" handout (at the end of this lesson and available at group.com/reproducibles.) Use the template to trace 30 text-bubble shapes on the poster board, and then cut them out. If you're pressed for time, kids who arrive early can help cut.

26

Tough-O-Meters

(about 10 minutes)

Form a circle, and give each preteen seven sticky notes. Have them each place their notes on the floor in a line in front of them.

SAY:

These sticky notes make up your tough-o-meters. What's a tough-o-meter, you ask? It's a device that measures how difficult it is for you to do something. The more bars—sticky notes—you display, the more difficult the task is for you. Let's try it.

Your parent asks you to clean your bedroom.

(Pause while kids select the number of bars to display.)

Your parent asks you to go out for ice cream.

(Pause to allow kids to adjust their tough-o-meters.)

Okay, now that we've practiced, let's use our tough-o-meters for something more challenging. I'm going to give you a series of situations you may have experienced where someone hurts or wrongs you. Use your tough-o-meters to measure how difficult you think it'd be to forgive the person in each situation.

Read the following statements, pausing after each one to give kids time to think and set their tough-o-meters.

- **Your little brother goes into your room without asking and breaks your MP3 player.**
- **You overhear your best friend gossiping about you in the cafeteria.**
- **Your friend borrows one of your books and forgets to return it.**
- **Your parent promised to take you to the movies but has to cancel because of work.**
- **Your friend cheats off your paper during a test without you knowing, and your teacher fails both of you.**

Have kids form pairs to discuss these questions.

ASK:

- **Tell about a time it was really *difficult* to forgive someone.**

27

- **Explain whether you've been *unable* to forgive someone for some-thing he or she did, and why.** (Be ready with your age-appropriate example if no one offers one.)

Read aloud Ephesians 4:32.

ASK:

- **What do you think it means to forgive others "as God through Christ has forgiven you"?**
- **What does it mean to you that God forgives you?**

SAY:

The Bible tells us a lot about forgiveness. Learning to forgive others is something that isn't always easy—no matter whether you're a kid or an adult. Let's dig in to find out how Jesus answered his disciples when they had questions about forgiveness.

PRESENT THE BIBLE FOUNDATION

Text a Parable

(about 25 minutes)

SAY:

Sometimes we can get tired of forgiving the same thing over and over and over. In Matthew 18, Jesus' followers were trying to figure out when they could quit forgiving someone who did the same bad thing over and over.

ASK:

- **Tell about a time you felt like the disciples because you had to keep forgiving someone for the same thing over and over.**

SAY:

One way Jesus responded to his friends was to teach them in parables or by using a simple spiritual lesson with a point. There are three main people in this parable Jesus told. There's a king, the first man who owed the king a lot of money—millions of dollars—and the second man who owed the first man a day's worth of pay.

Have kids form three groups, and give each group a Bible. Assign the following sections of Scripture to each group.

Group 1: Matthew 18:23-27

Group 2: Matthew 18:28-31

Group 3: Matthew 18:32-34

Allow time for groups to read their passages.

SAY:

Think about what happened in your passage of Scripture. Then with your group pretend that it's later that evening, after all the action in the parable is over. The debtor in the parable is exchanging text messages with a friend, trying to describe his eventful day.

Distribute markers and 10 dialogue bubbles to each group. Instruct groups to discuss what kinds of messages the debtor would send and then write them on the dialogue bubbles.

Give groups 10 minutes to work. Once time is up, have a representative from each group tell about its text messages in chronological order.

Have kids discuss the following questions in their groups.

ASK:

- What surprised you about what happened in Jesus' parable?
- Explain whether you think the king was right in what he did to the man who wouldn't forgive the other man's debt.
- Tell about a time you needed to forgive someone but didn't.

Read aloud Matthew 18:35, and then have the entire group discuss these questions.

ASK:

- Explain what you think the Bible passage means when it says to "forgive your brothers and sisters from your heart."
- Why do you think it matters to God whether you forgive someone from your heart or not?

SAY:

God wants us to forgive others—even people who do bad things to us over and over—because God forgives us over and over. It doesn't matter how much we think someone who did bad things to us owes us. Forgiving those things will never come close to how much or how many times God forgives us.

BUILD ON THE FOUNDATION

The Price of Forgiveness

(about 10 minutes)

SAY:

Let's take a closer look at the questions Peter asked Jesus about forgiveness.

Invite a willing preteen to read aloud Matthew 18:21-22.

SAY:

In Jesus' day, religious leaders thought if someone wronged you many times, you were only obligated to forgive that person three times. After three times, you were free to hold a grudge. Peter must've thought he was going above and beyond the call of duty by asking whether forgiving someone seven times was enough. Jesus' answer was probably a big surprise to him and anyone else listening.

ASK:

• Think about a person you've forgiven. What would be difficult about forgiving that person 70 times 7 times—or 490 times?

30

SAY:

The reality is, Jesus doesn't want us to keep track of how many times others wrong us. He was giving Peter a number so high that Peter would give up trying to get permission to stop forgiving others. Jesus knew the power of forgiveness. Listen to this verse.

Read aloud Hebrews 12:15.

ASK:
- What does this verse say will happen to us if we don't forgive others?
- Describe what it's like when someone is filled up with bitterness.

SAY:
When people wrong or hurt us, it's easy to focus on what we think they owe us or why we shouldn't forgive. Perhaps you're holding on to some bitterness and need to forgive someone. We're going to take time now to do that.

Give kids each a piece of tissue paper and a pen. Encourage them to go to a place in the room where they can pray quietly, asking God to show them anyone they need to forgive.

Allow four minutes of silence. During this time, place the bowl of water on the floor.

SAY:
When you're ready, write the name of the person you need to forgive on the tissue paper. Then come and place it in this bowl of water.

After everyone who wants to has placed tissue paper in the water, gather the kids in a circle around the bowl.

SAY:
Jesus' parable reminds us that we owe God more than anyone owes us—and he forgives us anyway. We can forgive others in the same way. As we forgive others from our hearts, all the hurt melts away—just like the tissue paper melts away. The bitterness melts away, and often the broken relationships melt away, too.

Read aloud Proverbs 17:9.

PRAY:
Dear God, thank you for forgiving us over and over. Help us remember the way you forgive us when others wrong or hurt us. Let us show your love by forgiving others. In Jesus' name, amen.

31

Dialogue Bubble Template

LESSON 4

We Serve Each Other

P reteens are usually ready to roll up their sleeves and get behind a cause they believe in. In fact, it's not uncommon to hear about preteens who've gained media attention for their ability to organize fundraising drives for causes they're passionate about. Such stories are encouraging and can give us a degree of hope for the future. At the same time, preteens often need reminders that serving is more than completing a task; it's an ongoing attitude. Use this lesson to help kids discover how Jesus became a servant to his disciples by performing one of the lowliest tasks imaginable—and how by doing so, he changed the way we view service to others.

Scripture Foundation

JOHN 13:3-8;12-17
Jesus set the example for his followers to humble ourselves.

PHILIPPIANS 2:6-8
Jesus is God—and he still humbled himself as a human.

MATTHEW 20:26-28
To be leaders, we must be servants like Jesus.

THIS LESSON AT A GLANCE

SEQUENCE	EXPERIENCES	SUPPLIES
SET THE FOUNDATION (about 10 minutes)	***Cookie-Dough Creation*** Kids gather supplies and then work together to make a messy cookie treat they'll serve to others.	• butter, brown sugar, flour, salt, vanilla extract, semisweet chocolate chips, water • measuring cups and spoons, mixing bowl, cookie sheet • wax paper • access to refrigerator • 1 copy of the "Cookie-Dough Treat Recipe" (at the end of this lesson) • antibacterial gel (optional)
PRESENT THE BIBLE FOUNDATION (about 25 minutes)	***The Greatest Servant*** Kids will clean each other's dough-covered fingers, read the account of the foot washing, and play a game.	• kid-friendly Bibles (preferably NLT) • wet wipes • pens • slips of paper, 1 per preteen
BUILD ON THE FOUNDATION (about 10 minutes)	***Behind the Scenes*** Kids will tour their church and serve their cookie-dough treats.	• kid-friendly Bible (preferably NLT) • cookies made in earlier activity • napkins • plates

Before the Lesson

SET THE FOUNDATION: *COOKIE-DOUGH CREATION*—Gather the ingredients and supplies, and find an appropriate place for kids to make the cookies. Depending on the size of your group, you may choose to have two or more groups making the recipe at once. Adjust your ingredients accordingly. Print a copy of the "Cookie-Dough Treat Recipe" (at the end of this lesson and available at group.com/reproducibles).

BUILD ON THE FOUNDATION: *BEHIND THE SCENES:* Make plans to tour your church in search of volunteers serving behind the scenes. Let other ministry leaders know ahead of time that you'll be bringing kids by to thank them and to deliver treats.

34

Cookie-Dough Creation

(about 10 minutes)

Have kids clean their hands and then gather around your workspace.

See page 8.

SAY:

Today we'll make special treats for hidden heroes in our church. These are people who serve others in ways that aren't always noticeable. We'll work together to make treats and then serve them as a way to say thank you.

Give one preteen the recipe, and have this person work with others to make the cookie-dough treats. Ensure that all kids get to help mix the ingredients with their bare, clean hands so everyone's fingers are eventually a sticky mess. Tell kids they can't wash, lick, or clean their hands in any way until you give the okay. Once the Cookie-Dough Treats are made and setting up in the refrigerator, gather kids together with their still-messy hands.

ASK:
- **Explain what it was like to make the cookies knowing you'll give them away.**
- **What do you think the point of serving others is if no one else notices?**
- **Tell about a time you served someone and no one noticed or said thanks.**

SAY:

In the Bible passage we're about to discuss, Jesus taught his friends about serving others. He taught them in an unusual way, and his disciples were uncomfortable. You might be uncomfortable right now with your sticky fingers. Let's see what Jesus taught his friends.

Don't allow kids to wash their hands yet.

35

The Greatest Servant

(about 25 minutes)

Explain to kids that Jesus washed his disciples' feet not long before he died. Jesus' followers had already heard him teaching about important things such as serving others. They knew servanthood was important to Jesus. He had also given the disciples opportunities to serve others publicly. Jesus encouraged his friends to do things like tell others about him. And he let them serve the fish and loaves to the crowd of 5,000 people.

SAY:

In Jesus' day, all roads were dirt roads, and people wore sandals. So whenever people went anywhere, they arrived with dirty feet. A household servant would show hospitality by washing guests' feet so they could enjoy the visit. The Bible tells us that not long before Jesus died, Jesus and his friends were having dinner but there was no servant to wash their feet. And none of Jesus' disciples volunteered to do the job.

ASK:

- **Tell about a time you served someone else, even if you felt uncomfortable.** (Be ready with your own age-appropriate example to share.)
- **What things can make it difficult for us to want to serve others?** Read aloud John 13:3-8 as shown below, doing the actions in parentheses:

Read verses 3-4. (Have kids sit in a circle with you standing in the middle.)
Read verse 5. (Hold out the package of wet wipes.)
Read verses 6-7. (Take out a wet wipe, and pretend to offer it to someone.)
Read verse 8. (Take the wet wipe back.)

ASK:

- **Explain whether you'd be willing to wash someone's stinky, filthy feet in this room right now.**
- **Why do you think Jesus, the King of kings, insisted on washing his friends' feet—even when they felt uncomfortable?**
- **What does this passage tell you about Jesus' relationship with his friends?**

36

SAY:

You and your sticky fingers must be really uncomfortable by now. Let's take a moment to serve each other.

Have kids form pairs, and then give each person a wet wipe. Have kids use the wet wipes to wash each other's fingers until they're clean. If you have an uneven number of kids, you can be someone's partner.

ASK:

- **What were you thinking when another person served you by cleaning your fingers?**
- **What do you think was uncomfortable for Jesus' friends about having him wash their feet?**

SAY:

Let's see what Jesus taught his friends about serving others after he washed their feet.

Make sure each pair has a Bible, and have kids open to John 13:12-17.

Read aloud verse 12. Then tell partners that they'll take turns reading each verse. One partner will read a verse, and the other partner will ask "Why?" The reading partner will answer, and the listening partner will ask "Why?" again. This will continue until the reading partner can think of no more answers. After each verse, have partners trade roles until the entire passage is read.

When everyone is finished,

ASK:

- **What did you learn about what Jesus thinks of service?**
- **After studying this Scripture, what do you think God wants our reason to be for serving others?**

SAY:

Let's look at this situation a different way.

Have kids form groups of three or four. Give each person a slip of paper and a pen. Tell kids to each think of and discuss one person they will choose to serve in the coming week. The catch is, kids must select an unexpected way to serve the person that'll be a challenge to the preteen. For instance, one preteen might choose to make a special, anonymous gift for another preteen at school who is consistently mean to him or her.

Allow time for groups to talk, and then have each preteen write on the slip of paper the name of the person they chose and the act of service. Have kids take home their papers as a reminder of their commitment to serve others in the coming week.

37

Behind the Scenes

(about 10 minutes)

Collect the Cookie-Dough Treats from the refrigerator, and have kids place one treat on each plate along with a napkin.

See page 8.

SAY:

We have some people in our church who are the greatest! Listen to what Jesus thinks of them.

Read aloud Matthew 20:26-28.

SAY:

Our church has so many people who serve others. They often serve behind the scenes and don't care whether anyone ever notices their service, just as Jesus instructed us. Let's thank them for serving like Jesus did and share our goodies.

Lead the kids around your church, looking for behind-the-scenes volunteers. Ask volunteers to explain to preteens what they do and why their behind-the-scenes service matters. Encourage kids to share their goodies and thanks with these volunteers. After the tour, return to your meeting space and let kids enjoy any leftover goodies.

PRAY:

Dear Jesus, thank you for giving us the life-changing example of serving others by washing your friends' feet. You showed us that no one is too important to serve. You also showed us that we can be servants, even when others don't notice what we do. Help us be more like you. In your name, amen.

Cookie-Dough Treat Recipe

INGREDIENTS:

1 stick of butter, softened

cup of light brown sugar, packed

1 cup of all-purpose flour

teaspoon of salt

tablespoon of vanilla extract

1 cup of semisweet chocolate chips

water

Yield:
36 cookies

DIRECTIONS:

1. Take turns combining the softened butter and the brown sugar in a medium mixing bowl USING YOUR HANDS.

2. Add the vanilla, and squish the mixture together for several minutes until it's light and fluffy.

3. Add the flour and salt to the butter mixture, and squish it together until it's well combined.

4. Add in water one tablespoon at a time until the dough reaches cookie-dough consistency.

5. Squish in the chocolate chips, and form the dough into 1-inch balls. Set them on a wax paper-lined cookie sheet.

6. Refrigerate cookies for 15 minutes or so to set up.

39

LESSON 5

We Don't Cause Each Other to Sin

The Bible has some very graphic illustrations in regard to causing others to sin. In Matthew 18:6, Jesus said there would be dire consequences for anyone who causes a little one who believes in him to fall into sin. He explained that "it would be better for you to have a large millstone tied around your neck and be drowned in the depths of the sea." Jesus takes this very seriously!

The Bible is clear that we're free from slavery to sin, but we must avoid using our freedom in Christ to cause our friends, family members, or others to sin. Use this lesson to show kids the huge responsibility we have as followers of Jesus to not cause others to sin.

Scripture Foundation

GALATIANS 5:13
Followers of Jesus don't use their freedom to sin.

ROMANS 14:13
Live in a way that doesn't cause others to sin.

MATTHEW 18:5-9
Sorrow awaits the person who causes others to sin.

THIS LESSON AT A GLANCE

SEQUENCE	EXPERIENCES	SUPPLIES
SET THE FOUNDATION (about 10 minutes)	***Mind Trips*** Kids will attempt to quickly solve brainteasers without making mistakes.	• none
PRESENT THE BIBLE FOUNDATION (about 25 minutes)	***Scripture Cartoons*** Kids will discover what the Bible says about causing others to sin as they play a game to discover how they can avoid tempting others to sin.	• kid-friendly Bibles (preferably NLT) • large sheets of paper • fine-tipped markers or colored pencils • paper
BUILD ON THE FOUNDATION (about 10 minutes)	***Lean on Me*** Kids will discover that we have connections with each other and that we can help or hurt others with those connections when it comes to sin.	• kid-friendly Bible (preferably NLT) • 1-foot lengths of yarn, 1 per preteen • scissors • modeling clay • table

Mind Trips

(about 10 minutes)

Welcome kids, and have them form a circle and sit down. Explain to kids that you'll ask a series of questions, and they'll respond by shouting out their answers as quickly as possible.

ASK:

- **Say "silk" three times really fast.** Pause for response. **What do cows drink?** (Water)
- **A farmer has 15 cows, and all but 8 die. How many does he have left?** (8)
- **John's mother has three children: one is named January and one is named February. What's the third one named?** (John)
- **Think of two words that rhyme with roast.** Pause. **What do you put in a toaster?** (Bread)

Thank kids for playing along.

ASK:

- **What was tricky about the questions I asked you?**
- **In what ways is this like or unlike when you have friends who try to trip you up by getting you to do things you know are wrong?**
- **Without naming names, tell about a time a friend tried to get you to do something you knew was wrong.**

SAY:

It's okay to make mistakes, like in this game, but sometimes we stumble and do things we know God says are wrong. That's sin. Today we'll discover that the Bible tells us not to cause each other to sin.

43

Scripture Cartoons

(about 25 minutes)

Form four groups. Give each group a Bible, a large sheet of paper, and fine-tipped markers or colored pencils. Assign groups the following Scriptures, and then have them draw a three-panel cartoon strip that depicts what they've read.

Group 1: Matthew 18:5-6

Group 2: Matthew 18:7

Group 3: Matthew 18:8

Group 4: Matthew 18:9

When groups are finished, bring them back together and have them share in chronological order their cartoon strips and explain what the Scripture said.

ASK:
- **What do you think it means to cause someone to fall into sin?**
- **Based on these verses, which is worse: sinning or causing others to sin?**
- **In what ways, if any, does this Bible passage change the way you look at your influence on others?**

SAY:
Remember, sin is doing things we know God says are wrong.
God doesn't want us to cause others to sin. Let's play a game to see what this is like.

Give kids sheets of paper, and have kids write down ways someone could cause another person to sin. Allow time. When kids finish writing, ask them to share. Then have them crumple their papers and toss them into the center of your meeting space. Invite kids to form pairs, and have partners stand across from each other with the paper wads and some distance between them. The partners on one side will be "Leaders" and those on the other side will be "Followers."

SAY:
The object of the game is to keep from "falling into sin." The wads of

paper represent the ways we cause others to sin. If you're a "Follower," you must lie down and grab the leg of your "Leader" partner. The Leader must drag you to the finish at the other side of the meeting space. Try to get to the end of the game without either of you touching any paper wads. Ready? Go!

If time allows, play the game again with partners swapping roles.

ASK:

- **What made this game easy or hard for you and your partner?**
- **What makes it easy or hard to not cause others to sin?**

Read aloud Romans 14:13.

ASK:

- **How do some people put stumbling blocks in front of others to make them sin?**

SAY:

Like it or not, God has put people in your life you can influence for good or bad. Let's see what the Bible says is a better way than causing others to sin.

BUILD ON THE FOUNDATION

Lean on Me

(about 10 minutes)

Have kids stand around a table, and give each person a 1-foot length of yarn and a small ball of modeling clay. Instruct kids to help each other tie the yarn loosely around their right wrists. Afterward, go around and tie the loose ends of yarn to the left wrist of the kids standing next to them. When finished, kids' hands will be connected to their neighbors' hands, making one large circle.

45

Tell kids that you'll call out a shape or an animal, and they'll have only 30 seconds to sculpt their clay into that shape. Start by calling out a shape or an animal, and have them begin sculpting. After 30 seconds, call time.

ASK:
• **What made it hard or easy to accomplish your mission?**
Cut the yarn between every other person, and play the game again.

ASK:
• **What was the difference between the first and the second game?**
Read aloud Galatians 5:13.

ASK:
• **Tell which of the ways we played the game best illustrates this verse, and why.**
• **What's love got to do with not causing others to sin?**

SAY:
Sometimes it's easy to stumble and fall into sin and lead others to stumble into sin, too. Instead, we can support and encourage each other to avoid sin. Lean on the person next to you as we pray.

PRAY:
Dear God, we love you and want to do what's right. We're weak, and it's easy to stumble and fall into sin. Talk to God silently about a sin in your life, and ask God to forgive you. (Pause while kids pray.) **Now talk to God silently about someone you may have caused to sin, and ask God to forgive you.** (Pause while kids pray.)

God, thank you for your forgiveness. Please teach us to rely on you and to support each other when we're tempted to sin. In Jesus' name, amen.

LESSON 6

We're Humble Toward Each Other

The Bible says that Jesus "made himself nothing" and took a humble position when he was born (NIV). Jesus then humbled himself even further by dying a criminal's death on the cross. If Jesus, God's only Son, was willing to humble himself to such an extent, we too can humble ourselves. In this highly competitive world, today's kids find themselves fighting to be the best on the field, in school, and in life. And sometimes that passion goes from a healthy pursuit of growing to arrogant thoughts and behaviors. Use this lesson to help kids discover what it means to be humble. Help them see that, like Jesus, we can humble ourselves as we serve others.

Scripture Foundation

LUKE 14:7-14
Jesus explains that whoever is humble will be exalted.

1 PETER 5:5
Followers of Jesus serve each other in humility.

2 TIMOTHY 3:1-5
Stay away from prideful people who don't love God.

PROVERBS 29:22-23
Humility brings honor.

THIS LESSON AT A GLANCE

SEQUENCE	EXPERIENCES	SUPPLIES
SET THE FOUNDATION (about 10 minutes)	***Top That*** Kids will try to top each other's stories as they discover that God wants us to be humble, not boastful.	• none
PRESENT THE BIBLE FOUNDATION (about 25 minutes)	***Seat of Honor*** Kids will draw and act out Bible verses to better understand God's view on being humble and prideful.	• kid-friendly Bibles (preferably NLT) • paper • pens
BUILD ON THE FOUNDATION (about 10 minutes)	***Acts of Humility*** Kids will act out ways to respond in humility to situations they face every day.	• none

Top That

(about 10 minutes)

Welcome kids, and have them sit in a circle. Explain that they'll play a game where they try to top each other's stories. One person may start with "I went roller skating last weekend." The next person in the circle will try to top that with something like "I went roller skating last weekend and met a celebrity." Continue around the circle until the story comes back to the person who started it or until kids can't come up with anything more outrageous.

Choose someone to start the story, and play as time allows.

ASK:
- **What did you like or dislike about trying to top others in this game?**
- **Tell about a time someone tried to top you by acting like they were better than you.**

SAY:
 We often avoid people who try to sound better than us or make it seem as if their lives are so much better than ours. When we try to top others, we're being prideful. This is the exact opposite of being humble.

ASK:
- **Tell about someone you think is humble.**
- **What are some ways you've learned to be humble?**

SAY:
Jesus told us to live humbly and demonstrated that with his actions. Let's dig in to learn more about what the Bible says about how we can be humble toward each other.

Seat of Honor

(about 25 minutes)

SAY:

The Bible tells of a time Jesus and his disciples were at a dinner. In Luke 14, Jesus gave some advice about how we can live in a humble way.

Form three groups. Give each group a Bible, a sheet of paper, and a pen. Have kids open their Bibles to Luke 14:7-14, and assign one section of the following Scripture to each group.

Group 1: Luke 14:7-9

Group 2: Luke 14:10-11

Group 3: Luke 14:12-14

Have someone from each group write the assigned verses on the top of the paper, and allow time for groups to look up and read their passages.

Then have groups read the verses one more time as they each think of a simple symbol that represents something they discovered or something that stood out to them. Encourage each member of the group to draw a symbol on the left side of the group's paper.

When groups are finished, have them trade pages with another group. Groups will look up and read the Bible passage written on the new paper and then write ways they think each symbol relates to the passage. Allow time for kids to work.

Afterward, bring kids back together and have each group share its verse, symbols, and what the symbols meant.

ASK:

• **What surprised you about Jesus' advice?**

• **What does this mean in verse 11: "Those who exalt themselves will be humbled, and those who humble themselves will be exalted"?**

• **Tell about a time you've seen what Jesus said in verse 11 happen in real life.**

50

SAY:

Let's talk some more about being humble by looking at the opposite mind-set, which is being prideful.

Have preteens give their own definition of what the word *pride* means. If positive or negative connotations seem to be taking over the discussion, ask for different points of view.

Form two groups. Assign one section of the following Scripture to each group, and make sure each group has a Bible.

Group 1: 1 Peter 5:5

Group 2: Proverbs 29:22-23

Have groups read their passages and listen for how the Bible describes pride. Afterward, have kids figure out how to pantomime the verse(s) for the other group so they can guess what's happening. Allow time, and then have groups take turns reading the verses aloud to each other.

ASK:
- **From your Scripture, tell about how God looks at being prideful.**
- **Explain whether you think there is or isn't a good form of pride.**
- **How can you avoid being prideful in a way that doesn't please God?**

SAY:

The Bible tells us that pride ends badly, while being humble brings honor. Just as Jesus humbled himself, we're called to be humble toward each other. Not only that, we may think, "Well, pride isn't that bad of a thing." Listen to the kinds of things that God says are just as bad as pride.

Read aloud 2 Timothy 3:1-5.

SAY:

Pride is a big issue to God. Rather than being prideful, God wants us to be humble toward each other.

51

BUILD ON THE FOUNDATION

Acts of Humility

(about 10 minutes)

Have kids form pairs.

Read the following scenarios one at a time. Invite one partner to tell a prideful response to the scenario and one partner to tell a humble response. After each scenario, have partners swap roles.

- **You got the only A in your class on your English paper.**
- **You scored the winning goal in your soccer game.**
- **You're the only one of your friends who received an invitation to a party.**

ASK:

- **Explain which was easier or harder to think of—a humble response or a prideful response.**
- **When is it hard for you to be humble toward others?**

SAY:

When we focus on ourselves instead of others, it's hard to be humble. Being humble can be hard, but Jesus served as the ultimate example of humility. Let's give thanks for that right now. Jesus came to earth as a servant even though he was God. That's humility!

Have kids find a place to silently pray to God, giving thanks for Jesus' example. Allow time for kids to pray silently before closing your time together in prayer.

PRAY:

Dear God, thank you for giving us Jesus as a perfect example of humility. Please show us where we're holding on to pride in our lives, and help us be humble toward each other. In Jesus' name, amen.

We Live in Harmony With Each Other

U nless they're in music class, preteens probably aren't using the word "harmony." But preteens do spend a lot of time in relationships that aren't always harmonious. From fights with friends to problems with parents, even the closest of preteen relationships can be filled with turmoil. God's Word has practical things to say about living in harmony and being peacemakers with each other. God provides simple instructions in the Bible for living in harmony, but these instructions aren't always easy to follow. You've got a fantastic opportunity to help preteens discover practical truths that will help them in every one of their relationships. Use this lesson to help preteens learn how to live in harmony with other people.

Scripture Foundation

ROMANS 12:16
Humility is the secret to harmonious living.

GALATIANS 5:26
Don't be conceited or jealous.

JAMES 3:16-18
Become a peacemaker.

THIS LESSON AT A GLANCE

SEQUENCE	EXPERIENCES	SUPPLIES
SET THE FOUNDATION (about 10 minutes)	**Smooth Moves** Kids will work together to roll a ball through a long paper tube.	• paper • ping-pong balls
PRESENT THE BIBLE FOUNDATION (about 25 minutes)	**Working in HARMONY** Kids will explore Scripture together, make a poster, and then discuss how they worked in harmony.	• kid-friendly Bibles (preferably NLT) • markers in at least 7 different colors • poster board or card stock
BUILD ON THE FOUNDATION (about 10 minutes)	**Live It Out** Kids will create and then solve puzzles to learn about harmony.	• poster board or card stock from previous activity • 2 pairs of scissors

Smooth Moves

(about 10 minutes)

Welcome kids, and tell them you're glad they came. Direct kids to an area with lots of open space, such as an outdoor lawn (weather permitting). Have preteens form groups of four. Give each person a sheet of paper and each group one ping-pong ball.

SAY:

We're going to play a game called Smooth Moves to experience harmony. *Harmony* means living together in peace and unity. With your group, stand in a straight line shoulder to shoulder. Each of you, make a tube out of your paper. Work together with your group to connect your paper tubes so that when the first person in line puts the ping-pong ball in his or her tube it'll run through your group's connected tube.

Allow time for kids to run the ball through their tubes a few times.

SAY:

Let's make it a little more complicated. Once the ball has passed on to the second person's piece of the tube, the first person in line will run to the end and reconnect. Keep going to see how far your group can roll the ball through your tube.

Cheer for kids as they work and play. After the game, bring kids together.

ASK:

- **What makes working together fun? challenging?**
- **Why do we sometimes have a hard time living in harmony with others?**

SAY:

Let's explore what each of us can do to live in harmony.

55

Working in HARMONY

(about 25 minutes)

Have preteens stay with their original groups of four. Give each group two Bibles, a piece of poster board or card stock, and markers. Have groups read Romans 12:16 and then put it in their own words. Allow one minute.

When finished, have one pair in each group read Galatians 5:26 and the other pair read James 3:16-18. Write the Bible references on a piece of poster board so groups can refer to them as needed. When pairs finish, have them take turns explaining the verses to the other air in their group. Allow four minutes.

ASK:
- **What did these Bible passages tell you about living in harmony?**
- **What does "selfish ambition" mean to you?**
- **Why do you think these things are important to God?**

SAY:
We've seen how the Bible tells us to live in harmony. Let's take a moment to think about what that looks like.

Write the word *HARMONY* vertically down the left-hand side of the poster board, and have groups do the same. Have groups assign a different color marker for each letter in *HARMONY* and evenly distribute the markers as best they can among their groups.

SAY:
Use the letters in the word *harmony* to describe what the Bible says about living in harmony in your relationships, starting with a word that starts with H, and then A, and so on down to Y. You might have to get really creative to fill in all the letters. When you come up with a word, write it on your group's poster board and draw a picture or symbol of what that looks like to you. Try to create a picture that represents harmony to your group.

Give groups time to complete the task. Provide assistance only to help kids understand their task, but let kids work together on their own to complete the activity. After five minutes, call time and have groups share about what they created.

SAY:

You may have thought you were just exploring Bible verses, but you were also doing a study in how groups work together.

ASK:

- In what ways do you think your group did or didn't work together in harmony during this activity?
- What could you have done to make your group work better?
- What are the benefits of Jesus' followers living in harmony with others?

SAY:

People who don't follow Jesus look at the church to see if God is making a difference in the lives of people who do attend church. When they see God's people fight, they might think that God isn't good. When people see us living peaceful, kind lives they see the difference that following Jesus can make in their relationships, too. Living in harmony with others can be challenging at times, but the benefits are worth it.

Read aloud James 3:18.

BUILD ON THE FOUNDATION

Live It Out

(about 10 minutes)

SAY:

You probably spend most of your time between home and school, so let's focus on those relationships.

Form two groups by drawing an imaginary line down the middle of your meeting space. Ask one group to think of a less-than-harmonious situation at school and the other group to do the same for a home situation. Have kids write their situation on the back of one of the pieces of *HARMONY* poster board. Give each group a pair

57

of scissors, and have them make a simple puzzle by cutting apart the picture. Have groups swap puzzles.

SAY:

Now your group will get to solve the puzzle you received. When you're finished, read the scenario. Discuss how someone could do his or her best to bring about harmony in that situation.

When groups are ready, have them choose a group representative to tell about their harmonious solution.

After the presentations,

ASK:

- **In what ways is living in harmony with others like or unlike putting a puzzle together as a team?**
- **Tell about a relationship you've had that didn't have harmony.**
- **What did you learn today that could help you in that puzzling relationship?**

SAY:

Relationships can be puzzling. We need to be careful to live in harmony with our friends and family. God wants us to live in harmony with each other, and he'll help us when we need it. Let's pray together now. As you feel comfortable, thank God for a discovery you made today or ask for wisdom on how to live in harmony with others.

Let kids pray spontaneously, and then close in prayer.

PRAY:

Dear God, you're so good. You've given us good relationships, and you've given us your Word to help us know how to live. Help us live in harmony with others. In Jesus' name, amen.

Allow kids to each take home a piece of their puzzle as a reminder that we're each a piece of God's plan, and God wants us to live in harmony so others can see the big picture—his love.

58

LESSON 8

We Accept Each Other

We live in a world of cliques, social clubs, and groups of people who share similar interests. And while it's fine to have like-minded friends, for preteens this can mean shunning outsiders and those who seem different. But it doesn't have to be that way. Jesus accepts everyone who wants to follow him. When we understand that Jesus accepts us, we can extend that same loving welcome to others. Use this lesson to help your kids discover that people may be different, but everyone is alike in a more important way: Jesus loves us all.

Scripture Foundation

ROMANS 15:7
Because Jesus accepts us, we accept each other.

MARK 2:15-17
Jesus models accepting others.

LUKE 10:25-28
Jesus challenges a religious expert's view on loving God and neighbors.

THIS LESSON AT A GLANCE

SEQUENCE	EXPERIENCES	SUPPLIES
SET THE FOUNDATION (about 10 minutes)	**Join the Club** Kids will create a make-believe club, including admission requirements.	• kid-friendly Bibles (preferably NLT) • paper • pens or markers
PRESENT THE BIBLE FOUNDATION (about 25 minutes)	**Greetings, Friends!** Kids will shake hands and discuss a series of questions while exploring Jesus' acceptance of others.	• kid-friendly Bibles (preferably NLT) • paper and pens • white glue • paper towels • plastic tablecloths • clean kitty litter (optional) • wet wipes
BUILD ON THE FOUNDATION (about 10 minutes)	**Chain of Acceptance** Kids will silently confess relational sins and then come together to celebrate their differences.	• quiet, reflective music and a music player (optional)

Join the Club

(about 10 minutes)

Welcome kids, and have them form groups of no more than four. Encourage kids to form groups with kids they might not know well. Give a sheet of paper and a pen or marker to each group.

SAY:

Work with your group to create a make-believe club. Come up with a purpose for your club and five membership requirements for those who want to join your club. For example, if your club is for space adventurers, one of the requirements could be that members have to recite all the names of the planets in our solar system.

Give groups three minutes to create their club and write membership rules.

Afterward, ask each group to present the name of its club and the membership rules. When everyone has shared, ask if there's anyone in the room who automatically qualifies to join any of the clubs. This could create a very poignant moment, as it's possible that no one will qualify to join any of the clubs or that everyone can make it into every club.

ASK:

- **In what ways was it easy or difficult to develop membership requirements for your club?**
- **What was it like knowing you could or couldn't get into a club you'd like to join?**
- **Tell about a time you felt accepted or included in a club or left out or excluded from a club.**

SAY:

Let's imagine for a moment that Jesus is starting a club. Have kids tell what they think Jesus' club might look like. **So what would the conditions be to join Jesus' club? In the book of Luke, an expert in religious law asked Jesus how to inherit eternal life. In this interaction, listen for five conditions for joining Jesus' club.**

61

Have someone read aloud Luke 10:25-28.

SAY:

We know that it's through Jesus that we inherit eternal life. Jesus was challenging this man to remember that his followers love God and love others.

ASK:

- What do you think about the conditions listed in these verses?
- Explain why you would or wouldn't want to join Jesus' club.
- What is significant about what these verses say about Jesus and acceptance?

SAY:

The Bible goes on to say that the expert questioned who the neighbors were that he had to love. Jesus wanted him and us to see that everyone is our neighbor. We tend to easily accept some people and ignore or even reject others, but that's not what Jesus does. Jesus accepts everyone and wants us to do the same. Let's explore that more now.

PRESENT THE BIBLE FOUNDATION

Greetings, Friends!

(about 25 minutes)

Give each preteen a Bible, a sheet of paper, and a pen. Have kids find a comfortable spot in the meeting space where they can sit that's away from others.

SAY:

Acceptance is something we all want, but sometimes we refuse to accept others. Today we're going to dig into a single verse in the Bible that speaks about acceptance.

62

Have kids write the following words in a column down the left-hand side of their paper: who, what, when, where, and how, and then have them turn to Romans 15:7. Explain to kids that you'll ask a question that relates to each one of these words.

SAY:

Before we start, I want you to write your name next to the word *who*, because we're going to see how this verse applies to you.

Have kids read Romans 15:7 and silently consider its meaning. After a minute, start asking these questions, one at a time. Pause after each one for kids to write.

ASK:

- **What does it mean to accept someone just as Christ accepts you?**
- **When is it hard to accept someone else?**
- **Where do you see yourself falling short of what is asked of us in Romans?**
- **How does God get the glory when we accept others?**

Have kids come back together and share what they discovered during this experience with the Bible. Afterward, collect the Bibles and spread the plastic tablecloths on the floor. Have kids form a big circle on the tablecloths.

SAY:

We're going to talk about Jesus' acceptance some more, but first let's play a handshaking game.

Starting with the person who happens to be closest to you, have kids count off by ones and twos around the circle. If there is an uneven number, join in the activity.

SAY:

Ones, turn your body so you walk clockwise. Twos, turn so you walk counterclockwise. If we've done this correctly, we'll still be in one big circle, but everyone should be facing someone else. Now we're going to try a fancy little walk-and-move. Reach out with your right hand and shake, but don't let go. Gently pull each other forward so you walk past each other's right shoulder.

Now reach out with your left hand and grab the hand of the next person in front of you. Take another step and you'll pass each other's left shoulder.

Now there's a new person in front of you, and you're reaching with your right hand.

63

Give assistance to any kids who need help understanding the movement. It may help to call up a preteen and demonstrate the motion. Have kids continue to keep the circle moving until you can see that everyone understands the movement.

SAY:

Stop. Stand right where you are, and listen for how Jesus accepted others in Mark 2:15-17.

Read aloud the Scripture. Explain that sinners are people who do things that God says are wrong, and that the Bible says everyone has sinned.

ASK:

- **The Pharisees and teachers of the religious law in Jesus' time called the tax collectors and sinners scum. In what ways have you felt either superior or like you were not as good as others?**
- **What do you think about how Jesus loves and accepts sinners?**

SAY:

I'm going to read the Bible passage one more time, except this time there's a catch: Ones, you're the Pharisees and Teachers. Twos, you're the Tax Collectors and Sinners. Before we start moving again, I have something for the Twos. If possible, lead the Twos outside of the meeting space. Bring out the white glue, and cover the kids' palms with it. If you cannot leave, have Ones close their eyes. (As an optional part of the activity, consider covering kids' glue-covered palms with clean kitty litter.)

Now move back to your place in the circle, and let's try our circle game one more time as I read from the Bible again.

Have kids start to move around the circle again as you slowly read Mark 2:15-17. Don't force kids who don't want to shake hands to do so. Bring the game to a stop when you're done reading the Scripture.

ASK:

- **What was it like shaking hands with someone from the other group?**
- **How is that like or unlike accepting some hard-to-accept people?**

SAY:

Jesus accepts all of us—yucky hands and all. He wants us to accept others in the same way.

Give kids wet wipes to clean their hands.

SAY:

You may not shake hands with others very often, but there are plenty of things you can do to demonstrate that you truly accept others. You can smile and say hello, invite someone to join your ballgame on the playground, or go to the park together after school. Be on the lookout for different ways you can help others feel accepted.

BUILD ON THE FOUNDATION

Chain of Acceptance

(about 10 minutes)

SAY:

We're all sinners. We blow it all the time. But we might not like to think about how we've sinned. Let's take some time to talk quietly to Jesus about how we've sinned in our relationships.

Ask kids to close their eyes and hold their fists in their laps.

SAY:

We can use our hands to show that we accept others, and we can use our hands to reject others. Your fists represent the times you haven't accepted others. Silently think about times you haven't accepted someone. Give that sin over to Jesus as you open your fists, one finger at a time. The goal is to end up with hands open to receive the forgiveness and the new friends Jesus wants to give you.

Play quiet, reflective music (optional) and have kids reflect. Give kids time to pray. Afterward, have kids stand up. Explain that you're about to ask some opinion questions, and their mission is to find someone with a different answer and then link elbows.

Read the following questions one by one, allowing time for kids to find others with different answers. Continue asking questions until everyone is in one big chain. If you get to the end of the list and everyone is still not linked up, come up with obvious questions, like "What color shirt are you wearing?"

- **What's your favorite sport or game to play?**
- **What's your favorite pizza topping?**
- **What's your best subject in school?**
- **How many brothers or sisters do you have?**
- **What's your favorite flavor of ice cream?**

SAY:

We are the body of Christ, and Jesus calls us to accept each other. To connect and receive one another. That's what we're doing right now! Let's end today by accepting each other through prayer. We'll start at this end of the chain and I'll say, "Jesus, you accept [name of person at the end of the line]**, and I do too!" We'll continue down the chain until the last person prays for me, and then I'll close in prayer.**

When the prayer reaches you, **PRAY:**

Dear God, thank you for accepting each one of us through Jesus Christ even though we're sinners. Thank you for Jesus' example that shows us how we can accept one another. In Jesus' name, amen.

LESSON 9
We Don't Judge Each Other

Judging others is part of being human. And kids, just like adults, are prone to judgment. This is especially true for preteens who are in the throes of insecurity. It's so easy for them to compare themselves with others—and judge those who don't measure up to their standards.

We often see judgment in schools, sports, friendships, and pop culture. This can be a hard concept for kids to grasp, but the Bible clearly steers us away from judging others. Jesus frees us from judgment through offering us understanding, acceptance, and forgiveness. Help kids see that it's sometimes easier to focus on the faults in others and not see how we're all more similar than we are different. Use this lesson to help kids learn not to judge each other.

Scripture Foundation

MATTHEW 7:1-5
Jesus tells his followers not to judge others.

JAMES 4:11-12
Jesus' followers don't judge each other.

ROMANS 2:1-4
When we judge others, we condemn ourselves.

JAMES 2:12-13
Mercy triumphs over judgment.

1 CORINTHIANS 4:3-5
You don't judge yourself; God judges you.

ROMANS 14:10-12
God is the ultimate judge.

JOHN 8:1-11
Jesus tells a woman's accusers to look at themselves first.

THIS LESSON AT A GLANCE

SEQUENCE	EXPERIENCES	SUPPLIES
SET THE FOUNDATION (about 10 minutes)	**Talent Show** Kids will discover what God's Word says about judging others while discovering how we often judge others every day.	• pens or markers • paper
PRESENT THE BIBLE FOUNDATION (about 25 minutes)	**Sticks...** Kids will work together to understand Jesus by putting what Jesus says into their own words.	• kid-friendly Bibles (preferably NLT) • paper • pens
BUILD ON THE FOUNDATION (about 10 minutes)	**And Stones** Kids will participate in an object lesson to realize how Jesus has forgiven them, and then they'll pray together.	• kid-friendly Bibles (preferably NLT) • a variety of soft balls, many sizes and styles

Talent Show

(about 10 minutes)

Welcome kids, and hand everyone a sheet of paper and a pen or marker.

SAY:

Today we'll begin with an improvised talent show. Each of you will take turns demonstrating a talent or a weird and wacky trick. It can be anything you want to show off as long as it's appropriate, it's not a repeat of someone else, and it's no more than 30 seconds. You'll be writing a score for each performance, but don't share what you wrote.

Encourage kids to keep things moving quickly and to have fun with their mini-performances. After each performance, keep the performer up front while the other kids write down the performer's name and a score from 1 to 10 on their papers. Remind kids not to share what score they wrote. Allow everyone who desires to participate, and then thank everyone for their efforts.

ASK:

- **In what ways was performing your talent in front of everyone easy or hard?**
- **Explain why it does or doesn't make a difference if people judge your performance.**
- **Tell about a time you felt judged by others.**

SAY:

Most people don't like it when others judge them. But for some reason, we keep on judging other people anyway. Today we're going to explore what God's Word says about judging others.

Sticks...

(about 25 minutes)

SAY:

To begin, let's take a look at what Jesus had to say about judging others.

Form four groups, and give each group a Bible, a sheet of paper, and a pen for any notes they want to jot down. Have groups read Matthew 7:1-5 and discuss these questions.

ASK:

- **What do you think about Jesus' response to judging others?**
- **Explain whether you think this system of judging and being judged is fair or not.**

Explain that in today's Bible study, kids will compare what Jesus said with other passages in the Bible. Assign one section of the following Scripture to each group.

Group 1: James 4:11-12

Group 2: Romans 2:1-4

Group 3: James 2:12-13

Group 4: 1 Corinthians 4:3-5

Allow time for groups to read their Bible passages, and have them answer the following questions based on their passages.

ASK:

- **What does God think about judging?**
- **What does God want us to do instead of judging?**

Afterward, have kids paraphrase to the other groups what they read and report what they talked about on how God views judging.

SAY:

As we look at judging others, we can see that God is the judge, not us.

Read aloud Romans 14:10-12.

And Stones

(about 10 minutes)

Have kids gather in front of you, leaving a little space between you and the group. Show everyone your collection of balls.

SAY:

In Bible times, stoning was a form of punishment; a death penalty. People would corner the accused and throw stones at them, often continuing until they died. We're not going to throw stones today, but I'll admit I've done something wrong.

Tell everyone a personal story of a time you've sinned; for example, a time you told a lie.

SAY:

Imagine that the punishment for this crime is stoning. However, instead of using real stones, you'll use balls. In just a few minutes, you can throw the balls right at me. After all, I've sinned. It was a terrible, horrible thing to do. Justice must be served, and I must pay the price.

Get your kids really stirred up about this, and you'll likely see them become very eager to get their hands on the balls and start throwing.

Paraphrase John 8:1-11 for the kids (the story of the woman at the well), and ask a willing preteen to read aloud John 8:7. Have kids repeat it.

ASK:

- **In what ways is our situation like or unlike what we just heard?**
- **What's surprising about the way Jesus handled the situation?**
- **In what way is Jesus' attitude about judging others like or unlike your own?**

Remind kids about your sin and the punishment to be given. Based on the discussion, have kids decide whether they'd like to continue or sit down. Allow those who want to sit down to do so. If anyone remains standing, ask them why they want to continue. Thank kids for their honesty, and use this opportunity to explain that while there are still consequences for our actions, Jesus forgives us for our sins. Collect the balls.

71

ASK:

- Think about some of the things Jesus has forgiven you for doing or even thinking. In what ways can you share that forgiveness with other people?

SAY:

When we're tempted to judge others, we can remember to look at ourselves before looking down on people who are different from us. Even when people do wrong, we can remember how Jesus forgave us all and then we can forgive them as well. Let's pray together.

PRAY:

Dear God, thank you so much for sending Jesus to forgive us. Thank you for showing us a great example of how to love and forgive others. Please help us as we try to love and forgive others, too, instead of judging them. In Jesus' name, amen.

LESSON 10

We're United With Each Other

Most preteens feel a need to belong and an urge to unite with others. The great news is they can fulfill that need by coming alongside other followers of Jesus. The unity of his followers was one of Jesus' highest priorities. Christ prayed fervently for our unity the night of his betrayal. Jesus knew that if his followers could remain united in love, they'd provide a glimpse of his love to others. Help your kids see what's really at stake when followers of Jesus argue. We tear at the body of Christ and put unnecessary obstacles in others' path to following Jesus. Use this lesson to help kids discover how God's love unites us all.

Scripture Foundation

1 CORINTHIANS 1:10-17
A church divided discovers that Jesus helps us be united in mind and thought.

EPHESIANS 4:4-6
Jesus' followers are united together as one through God.

1 PETER 3:8
Jesus' followers love one another and are like-minded.

THIS LESSON AT A GLANCE

SEQUENCE	EXPERIENCES	SUPPLIES
SET THE FOUNDATION (about 10 minutes)	**Stronger Together** Kids will experience strength in numbers by breaking toothpicks and comparing the strength of one vs. many.	• wooden toothpicks
PRESENT THE BIBLE FOUNDATION (about 25 minutes)	**All for One...** Kids will discover what God's Word says about unity in Christ by reading Bible passages aloud and working though church quarrels.	• kid-friendly Bibles (preferably NLT) • poster board • tape • marker • paper • pens • several concordances
BUILD ON THE FOUNDATION (about 10 minutes)	**And One for All** Kids will work together to create human machines to illustrate the importance of being united for one purpose.	• none

Stronger Together

(about 10 minutes)

Welcome kids, and give each person one toothpick.

SAY:

Today we're going to begin with a contest of strength, but we're all going to do it together. Go ahead and break your toothpick in half.

After everyone has broken their toothpick, hand two toothpicks to each person. Have them stack the two toothpicks together and try to break them in half. Hand out more toothpicks, and have everyone keep adding to the number of toothpicks they try to break until the stack becomes too strong to break. Give kids time to do this and report on how many toothpicks they were able to break at one time.

ASK:

- **Why was it harder to break the toothpicks as the numbers grew?**
- **What are some things that are weak by themselves but get stronger with more of them together?** (Some ideas are teams, packs of animals, or spaghetti noodles.)

SAY:

Lots of things—sometimes even people—aren't always very strong on their own. But when we're united, we can become very strong— almost impossible to break apart. Let's check out what God's Word says about how God wants us to be united.

LESSON 10: We're United With Each Other

All for One...

(about 25 minutes)

SAY:

The Bible tells about a church whose people were quarreling and arguing.

The passage we're about to read comes from a letter Paul sent to the arguing church.

Give each person a Bible, and have kids find 1 Corinthians 1:10-17. Have kids start reading the passage aloud when you point to them, but point to different kids at different times so there's no unity.

ASK:

• **Whoa! What was that like?**

Have kids read the Scripture again, but with one person reading each verse.

ASK:

• **How was reading the Scripture different this time compared with the first time?**

• **What do people in churches fight about today?**

As kids name things, write each one on a sheet of poster board taped where all the kids can see it.

Then have kids form pairs. Assign one of the quarrel topics to each pair (you don't have to cover all the topics, and you can repeat topics if you have more pairs than topics.)

Have each pair think of what God would say to each church about their quarrel topic. Encourage kids to use a concordance to find verses that would address the issue, and have them use pen and paper to take notes. After kids have had enough time, bring them back together and ask each pair to report its findings to the rest of the kids.

SAY:

Sometimes followers of Christ seem to forget the most important things that we all have in common and that unite us together. Instead, we

concentrate on differences and focus on the smaller things that can lead us to argue. Let's see what God's Word says about the important things that help unite us together.

Have kids find Ephesians 4:4-6, and have a preteen read these verses aloud. Turn over the poster board so you have a clean side for the next activity.

SAY:

These verses tell us some important things that all Christians have in common, such as every Christian being "called to one glorious hope" and having "one Lord" and "one faith." Let's use some of the things mentioned in this Scripture to write a cheer that could encourage Christians to live in unity.

Encourage everyone to work together to create a unity cheer. Have kids explain which sections of the passage stood out to them and choose the ones they want to use to create their cheer. Have kids use the poster board to write down the cheer they come up with. For example: *All for one and one for God/We're united like one bod!/If we're divided, then we'll fall/We're united, God is over us all!*

When they've finished the cheer, have kids chant it together.

SAY:

God wants his people to unite with each other. We're never going to agree on everything, but when it comes to the most important things, we do agree! Those are the things we can show the world! Let's discover more about why God wants us to be united.

BUILD ON THE FOUNDATION

And One for All

(about 10 minutes)

Form large groups of about 10. It's okay if there's only one group.

SAY:

Work with your group using your bodies to form an appliance or machine. Every person in your group must participate. For example, you could decide to form a car, with some acting as the wheels, the steering wheel, windshield wipers, and so on. The important thing is that everyone participates and that you all work together in unity.

Give kids a few minutes to figure out their machines, and then have them present to the group. Congratulate them for their participation, and lead the group in a round of applause.

ASK:

- What made this activity easy or challenging?
- What difference does it make in a real machine whether all the parts are working together or not?
- What difference does it make in God's kingdom if we're united or not?

SAY:

We're called to be one body. Just like a machine, we're made up of different parts, and we each have our own unique purpose. But it's when we come together as one that we can do some amazing things for God. Let's come together as one now to talk to God.

Have kids form a circle and huddle together to show their unity.

PRAY:

Dear God, help us to unite with each other. Help us remember that we all have you in common, and that's what's most important. Thank you for your love. In Jesus' name, amen.

LESSON

We Bear Each Other's Burdens

The idea of sharing each other's burdens can be sticky and scary at times. When should we help and when shouldn't we? When does sharing burdens become rescuing and enabling? And where can we go when we're feeling overwhelmed by our own burdens? Challenge kids with these kinds of questions, and open them up to the idea of sharing responsibility for each other. Throughout this lesson, kids will have the opportunity to think about the burdens we share, the burdens we carry, and how we can rely on Jesus to be the ultimate bearer of our burdens.

Scripture Foundation

GALATIANS 6:1-3
We can gently and humbly help others with their burdens.

GALATIANS 6:4-5 (NIV)
Each person must carry his or her own load.

MATTHEW 11:28-29
Jesus asks those who are weary to come to him.

THIS LESSON AT A GLANCE

SEQUENCE	EXPERIENCES	SUPPLIES
SET THE FOUNDATION (about 10 minutes)	**Burden Books** Kids will create heavy burden bins by writing down a current burden and taping it to a book.	• 2 bins • hardcover books (or other heavy items), 1 per preteen • pens • index cards • tape
PRESENT THE BIBLE FOUNDATION (about 25 minutes)	**Burden Bucket Brigade** Kids will discover how to share their burdens by creating a bucket brigade to move a pile of burden books.	• kid-friendly Bibles (preferably NLT) • 1 NIV Bible • books and bins from the previous activity
BUILD ON THE FOUNDATION (about 10 minutes)	**Death to Burdens** Kids will take their heavy burden bins to the cross, leave them, and replace them with Jesus' light yoke.	• kid-friendly Bible (preferably NLT) • books and bins from the previous activity • large cross • quiet, reflective music and music player (optional)

Before the Lesson

SET THE FOUNDATION: *BURDEN BOOKS*— Using a looped piece of tape, attach an index card to each book or heavy item. If you have fewer than 10 kids, make extra books with burdens taped to them so you'll have at least 10 burden books.

BUILD ON THE FOUNDATION: *DEATH TO BURDENS*— Prop a large cross up against a wall in your meeting space near one of the empty bins from the "Burden Books" activity.

80

SET THE FOUNDATION

Burden Books

(about 10 minutes)

Welcome kids as they arrive.

SAY:

A burden is a load we bear, usually a heavy one. Some burdens are physical, such as a heavy load of books you have to carry in your backpack. Other burdens aren't visible because they're emotional, spiritual, relational, or mental. Think of a burden you've had to deal with on your own or one you've helped a friend overcome. Maybe it's dealing with people in your family not getting along, having a hard time in one of your classes, or struggling to resolve an issue with a friend. It can be anything that's been hard for you to carry.

Give kids a minute to think about a burden, and then give them each a book with an index card taped to it and a pen. Have kids write their burden on their index card, instructing them not to put their names on the cards.

Collect all the books in one bin. Place the full bin at one end of the room and the empty bin at the other end of the room.

SAY:

Sometimes we carry our burdens around with us. Today you'll have to carry your burdens across this room and place them in the empty bin.

Have kids line up. Challenge kids to take turns running from the full bin to the empty bin carrying all the burdens—without using the bins. Allow every preteen a chance to run.

ASK:

- **What was difficult about handling these burdens by yourself?**
- **What's difficult about handling burdens in life by ourselves?**

SAY:

God doesn't want us to carry overwhelming burdens by ourselves. He wants us to share each other's burdens every day. Let's dig into the Bible to find out more about bearing each other's burdens.

81

LESSON 11: We Bear Each Other's Burdens

Burden Bucket Brigade

(about 25 minutes)

SAY:

In our game, we carried heavy burdens. In the book of Galatians, Paul gives us some helpful instructions about bearing one another's burdens.

Form groups of four, and give each group a Bible. Have groups read Galatians 6:1-3 and answer the following questions.

ASK:

• What do these verses say about burdens?

• Why does it take gentleness and humility to help each other?

Invite one preteen to read aloud Galatians 6:4-5 from an NIV version of the Bible.

ASK:

• How is this different from what we just read in Galatians 6:1-3?

• Name some burdens that people need to carry on their own— paying their bills, for example.

• What are some burdens people need help coping with—living with cancer, for example.

SAY:

Galatians 6:2 says, "Share each other's burdens, and in this way obey the law of Christ." Let's see what that's like.

Have kids form a line between the two bins.

SAY:

You're now a bucket brigade. A bucket brigade is a group of people in a line that moves objects from one place to another by passing them from person to person. Your job is to get your burdens from this bin one at a time and move them down your line and into the bin at the end. Each time a burden comes into your hands, feel the weight of it and read

82

what's on the index card. This isn't a race, so take your time and pay attention to each burden. Ready? Go.

After they've played, thank kids for participating.

ASK:

- In what ways did the brigade make carrying the burdens easier or harder? How is this like or unlike sharing burdens at home and school?
- Which version of the game was most like Galatians 6:1-3? Explain.
- Tell about a burden you saw as you passed burdens among one another.
- Choose one of those burdens, and tell how you could help someone bear it.

SAY:

Some burdens are hard to bear alone, and we need other people to help us with them. But as we help others, we need to make sure we're not weighed down by burdens ourselves. Jesus says we can come to him with all our burdens, so let's talk more about the ultimate burden-lifter.

BUILD ON THE FOUNDATION

Death to Burdens

(about 10 minutes)

Give everyone a book from the previous activity. Demonstrate how to hold it in the palms of your hands while keeping both arms straight out in front of you.

SAY:

Many of us have days or weeks when we're weary and tired. Maybe it's because we're physically tired, or maybe it's because we're carrying a lot of burdens.

83

ASK:

• Tell about a time you were tired and felt like you couldn't go on.

Read aloud Matthew 11:28-29.

ASK:

• What does rest from a heavy burden mean to you?

• What do you think about Jesus' offer?

Direct kids' attention to the cross and the empty bin.

SAY:

This cross reminds us of Jesus' sacrifice for us. He died for us because he loves us. His death has also made forgiveness for our sins possible. Also in front of you is our bin for burdens. Take a few minutes to talk to God about the burdens in your life, and ask him to help you trade them in for God's rest. When you're ready, come place the burden book you're holding in the bin. When you leave it there, ask God to replace your burden with his rest and peace.

Play quiet, reflective music (optional) while kids pray.

SAY:

Jesus wants us to bear each other's burdens. Luckily, Jesus is ready to give us rest for our burdens. Let's thank him now.

PRAY:

Dear Jesus, thank you for allowing us a chance to help each other with our burdens. Show us when we need to give our burdens over to you and embrace your rest. In your name, amen.

Prayer is a pretty abstract concept to grasp. For preteens, though, who are moving from concrete thinking to abstract thinking, prayer is a great topic to dive into. Some kids this age may wonder why we pray if an all-knowing and all-powerful being knows what we're going to say before we even say it. Or they may think that prayer is individualistic verbal thank-you cards and lists of requests. Prayer is so much more than that! Help kids realize that prayer is a way to talk with God and spend time with him. When we pray, not only does God listen, but he also shows up in powerful ways. Use this lesson to help kids learn that God wants us to pray with and for each other.

Scripture Foundation

JAMES 5:13-18
James encourages Christians to pray for each other and states that prayer has "great power."

MATTHEW 18:19-20
Jesus says that when his followers pray together, he's with them.

PSALM 65:1-5
God is our hope and faithfully answers our prayers.

THIS LESSON AT A GLANCE

SEQUENCE	EXPERIENCES	SUPPLIES
SET THE FOUNDATION (about 10 minutes)	***Communication Code*** Kids will talk about how we communicate over long distances and learn how to use Morse code to send short messages to each other.	• copies of the "Morse Code" handout (at the end of this lesson and available at group.com/reproducibles), 1 per person
PRESENT THE BIBLE FOUNDATION (about 25 minutes)	***Prayer Is...*** Kids will write down and compare their thoughts about prayer with what the Bible says about prayer.	• at least 2 kid-friendly Bibles (preferably NLT) • large writing surface such as a poster board, chalkboard or whiteboard • markers, chalk, or dry-erase markers (depending on surface) • bowl of water • small plastic cups • spoons • small towel
BUILD ON THE FOUNDATION (about 10 minutes)	***Prayer Wall*** Kids will write short prayers for each other, friends, or loved ones on sticky notes and stick them on a prayer wall.	• pens • pads of sticky notes • paper and marker (optional)

Before the Lesson

BUILD ON THE FOUNDATION: *PRAYER WALL* — Gather enough pens for everyone to have one and also a few pads of sticky notes. Have a blank wall or bulletin board area prepared where kids can place their sticky-note prayers, or make a "Prayer Wall" sign and post it near where the prayers will be placed.

Communication Code

(about 10 minutes)

Welcome kids, and have them form a circle. Spend time connecting with the kids in your group by having them share a time they saw God show up during their week.

SAY:

We communicate with people in lots of different ways. What are some ways we talk with people who live far away?

Allow kids to share their ideas.

SAY:

Before there was video chat, texting, email, or even telephones, people used something called Morse code to communicate. Does anyone know what Morse code is?

Allow kids to share. Give each person a copy of the "Morse Code" handout, pointing out the system of dots and dashes. If you have kids who know how Morse code works, allow them to explain it to the rest of the kids. If not, explain to kids that Morse code is a system of long and short sounds that represent letters. Spend a couple of minutes having kids clap and snap out some of the letters one at a time, using snaps for dots and claps for dashes.

SAY:

Let's see how well we can send and receive messages in Morse code. We're going to clap and snap out some words in Morse code one letter at a time. Let's try to figure out what words we're trying to send to each other.

Starting with the preteen to your left, have him or her think of a short word to clap out for the rest of the group to guess. Continue around the rest of the circle. When it comes back to you, finish by clapping out the word *pray* for kids to guess.

SAY:

We had fun communicating with one another! We really had to listen well.

87

ASK:

- **What surprised you about talking to others in Morse code?**
- **In what ways do you think using Morse code is like or unlike talking to God?**

SAY:

We're going to look at what the Bible has to say about prayer, but first let's discuss what we think we know about prayer.

PRESENT THE BIBLE FOUNDATION

Prayer Is...

(about 25 minutes)

Set out the poster board and markers (or another writing surface and supplies).

SAY:

We all have ideas about what prayer is or why we pray or how we pray. For the next few minutes, let's take turns writing at least two things you each think of that describe prayer.

Encourage kids to add to the collage of words and phrases. It's okay if kids write the same things as other kids. After a couple of minutes, discuss with kids what they wrote. Give some of the kids an opportunity to share about what they wrote.

Form two groups, and give each group a Bible. Have one group read James 5:16 and the other group read Matthew 18:19-20. Give groups time to talk about what their verses say about prayer. Then have kids pair up with someone from the other group. Have partners share their Bible passage and any discoveries they made.

Afterward, allow kids to add to the collage using their new discoveries as inspiration. If any kids propose a change, have them explain why they want to change something. Only add to the board, though; don't take anything away. The purpose of this activity isn't to have a correct definition of prayer written down, but to facilitate discussion about what kids think about prayer.

88

ASK:
- What do you think about the claims made in these verses?
- What sort of great power do you think prayer has?
- What's the point of praying *with* each other? praying *for* each other?

Set out a bowl of water. Then give each pair a plastic cup and spoon. Have pairs think of things they'd like to pray for together. For each thing they come up with, have them put a spoonful of water into their cups. Call time before cups fill more than halfway.

SAY:
With each of you using just one index finger, work together to lift the cup so it's above your heads.

If some water spills, that's okay. Offer a small towel, and move on with the activity.

ASK:
- What was this activity like for you?
- In what ways is this activity like or unlike what happens when we pray for each other? with each other?

SAY:
Prayer isn't just about me, myself, and God; God wants us to pray for each other and with each other. And God is faithful to answer our prayers.

Read aloud Psalm 65:1-5.

BUILD ON THE FOUNDATION

Prayer Wall

(about 10 minutes)

SAY:
In Jesus' day, there was a huge temple, or church, where people from all over came to worship God. In the year 70 AD, the temple was

destroyed. Part of one of the walls that surrounded that temple survived and still exists today. Some people call it the Wailing Wall. Just like in Jesus' time, people from far and wide come to see this ancient wall. One of the things people do at the Wailing Wall is write prayers on paper and put those prayers in cracks that are in the wall. We're going to make our own prayer wall as we finish up today.

Hand out pens, and make sure every preteen has several sticky notes. Let kids know that they'll spend a few minutes praying for each other as well as for other friends and loved ones. Encourage kids to write their prayers on sticky notes and then place those notes on the area you've designated for the "Prayer Wall."

After 10 minutes, collect the pens and sticky notes. Close your time together in prayer.

PRAY:

Dear God, sometimes we can feel you so close to us and sometimes it feels like you're far away. We thank you, God, that no matter what's going on in our lives we can talk to you and you hear us. God, thank you for the friends and family you've given us. We ask that you'd hear our prayers for them. In Jesus' name, amen.

Morse Code

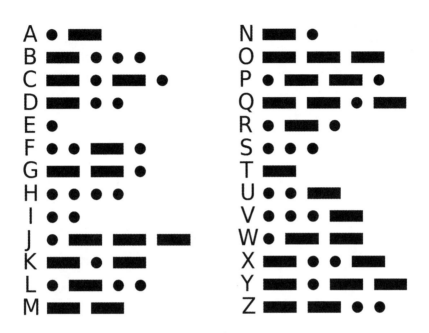

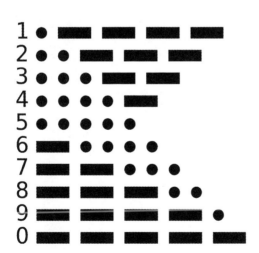

LESSON 12: We Pray for Each Other

LESSON **13**

We Encourage Each Other

Encouragement plays an important part in our lives. It brings out the best in people, and encouragement gives hope for the future. Encouragement affirms our identity in Christ and guides us toward spiritual growth and maturity. When kids begin to love others by becoming Christ-like encouragers, they see themselves as integral parts of God's great, big plan. That's important for preteens who are forming their identities. Use this lesson to help kids discover the value of encouragement and look for ways they can regularly encourage others.

Scripture Foundation

HEBREWS 3:7-13
We encourage each other to avoid becoming hardhearted by sin's deceitfulness.

HEBREWS 10:24-25
God wants us to think of ways to motivate one another to acts of love and good works.

THIS LESSON AT A GLANCE

SEQUENCE	EXPERIENCES	SUPPLIES
SET THE FOUNDATION (about 10 minutes)	***Nutty Stacks of Encouragement*** Kids will experience the value of encouragement in this nutty stacking game.	• zip-top plastic bags filled with 8 large metal nuts and 1 craft stick, 1 bag per 2 preteens • timer
PRESENT THE BIBLE FOUNDATION (about 25 minutes)	***Becoming an Encourager*** Kids will dig into Scripture and discover what it means to encourage others as they play a blindfolded game, give high fives, and build towers of encouragement.	• kid-friendly Bibles (preferably NLT) • wet wipes • lotion • very fine red glitter • download of the TobyMac song "Speak Life," a music player, and copies of the song's lyrics (available online)
BUILD ON THE FOUNDATION (about 10 minutes)	***Encouragement Slips*** Kids will create a poster of encouragement slips that'll help them encourage family and friends throughout the week.	• copies of the "Be an Encourager!" handout (at the end of this lesson and available at group.com/reproducibles), 1 per preteen • several pairs of scissors • crayons and markers

94

Nutty Stacks of Encouragement

(about 10 minutes)

Welcome kids, and have them form two teams. Have the teams sit on opposite sides of your meeting space facing each other.

SAY:
We'll take turns competing today. In just a moment, I'll give everyone on Team One a bag with a craft stick and some metal nuts. Each of you will hold on to one end of the craft stick. When we're ready to begin, I'll set the timer for one minute and we'll see if each of you can stack eight nuts on the end of your craft stick before time runs out. While Team One competes, Team Two will be completely silent. Don't say anything or react in any way. You're going to sit still like stone statues—no smiles or expressions of any kind.

Distribute the bags of supplies to Team One. Have kids place their craft sticks in one hand and when everyone's ready, start the timer. Make sure everyone on Team Two remains completely silent and watches without expression.

SAY:
Let's try this game again, only this time I'm going to give both teams a job. Team Two will have the same supplies and play the game the same way, but this time Team One will be encouragers! Team One, give Team Two suggestions and encourage them to keep trying and not give up.

Ask Team One to hand over the bags of supplies to Team Two. Have the Team Two kids place their craft sticks in one hand and when everyone's ready, start the timer. Make sure kids on Team One encourage Team Two as they compete.

ASK:
• **What difference did encouragement make in this game?**
• **What difference does encouragement make for you when you're trying to do something difficult?**

95

SAY:

Encouragers speak or act in a way that gives someone else courage to keep going, giving the person hope for the future. Let's see what we can learn about encouragement from a popular Christian song.

PRESENT THE BIBLE FOUNDATION

Becoming an Encourager

(about 25 minutes)

Give kids copies of the lyrics to TobyMac's song "Speak Life" from the album *Eye on It.* Have kids follow along with the words as they listen to the song.

ASK:

- **What does this song have to do with encouragement?**
- **What does the chorus say about why people need encouragement?**
- **Do you agree or disagree with the words in this song?**

SAY:

The Bible tells about the Israelites who continued to harden their hearts and rebel against God.

Read Hebrews 3:7-11.

SAY:

God had a strong message for Christians so they wouldn't be like the Israelites who rebelled against God.

Have kids form pairs, and give each pair a Bible. Have pairs read Hebrews 3:12-13 and then answer these questions in their pairs.

ASK:

- **According to these verses, why is encouragement important to our relationship with God?**
- **How is encouragement like "speaking life" to people's hearts?**

While kids work, open your Bible to Hebrews 10:24-25 and keep it nearby. Apply lotion to your hands and secretly sprinkle fine red glitter all over your hands. Bring kids back together and have them report to everyone their discoveries.

Read aloud Hebrews 10:24-25.

SAY:

God calls us to encourage one another, and that's "speaking life." Let's practice speaking life to one another. Go around the room and encourage each other with high fives and encouraging words. Once you've received a high five, you can walk up to someone else, encourage him or her with kind words, and give a high five. Let's pass along as many high fives and words of encouragement as we can in the next two minutes!

Give kids about two minutes to give as many high fives and kind words as they can. Make sure that you give as many high fives as you can, too. The glitter on your hands will be passed around with each high five. Afterward, have kids look at their hands. Explain that you had red glitter on your hands to start the activity.

ASK:

- **What's so contagious about encouragement?**
- **In what ways would our world be different if we all encouraged one another?**

Pass around wet wipes so kids can clean the glitter off of their hands.

BUILD ON THE FOUNDATION

Encouragement Slips

(about 10 minutes)

SAY:

Maybe you think it feels strange to tell your parents they've done a good job, or you're worried your friends will think it's weird if you encourage them to make the right choice. To help those opportunities to

97

encourage others go more smoothly this week, we're going to make a poster of encouragement slips.

Give each person a copy of the "Be an Encourager!" handout, and have available crayons, markers, and scissors.

SAY:

This handout is full of encouragements you can give your family and friends this week.

Have kids color and decorate the title on the side of the page and then cut on all the broken lines to create a fringe of encouragement slips. There are two blank slips included so kids can each write thei b r own encouragements.

SAY:

When you get home, hang this up somewhere in the house so everyone can see it. The refrigerator would be a great place! When you see someone who needs to be encouraged, tear off the appropriate slip and give it to the person!

When everyone has finished, close your time together in prayer.

PRAY:

God, you're the ultimate encourager! Because of your perfect example, we're able to love and encourage others. Help us be on the lookout for ways to be encouragers and speak the words others need to hear. In Jesus' name, amen.

Be an Encourager!

Keep trusting God! He's in control!

Wow! Your determination is amazing!

Congratulations! You did it!

I'm thankful for the way you support me.

Your faith in God encourages me.

Slow down and take a deep breath!

I believe in you!

God loves you even more than I do!

99

Give kids a foundation to build on!

▶ ISBN 978-0-7644-7066-0 • $19.99

13 Most Important Bible Lessons for Kids About God

Children's ministry leaders have been asking for an effective way to teach kids the foundational truths of the Christian faith. *13 Most Important Bible Lessons for Kids About God* is the answer. This practical and engaging resource will draw children closer to Jesus and help them get a firm grip on God's truths. These 13 Bible-packed lessons enable upper-elementary kids to experience, grasp, and embrace the fundamentals of their faith.

Each lesson is designed for upper-elementary kids, and includes:

- Lesson at glance
- Relational applications
- Scripture foundations
- Opener
- Closing prayer

You and your kids will get a solid understanding of what's really true about God so they can build their faith. And you, the teacher, will be fully equipped to tackle tough questions and encourage children every step of the way.

For more information:
Go to group.com or visit your favorite Christian retailer!

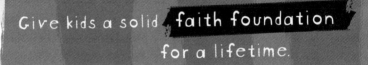

WHeN you HaVe KiDS of aLL aGes in one CLaSSRooM

Each book in this best-selling series includes 13 fun, Bible-based lessons for kids. You'll discover interactive programs filled with creative ideas for mixed-age classes. They work great for small churches, larger churches with multi-age classes, midweek programming, and any time you want to teach meaningful Bible lessons to kids of different ages—in the same class. You'll be ready no matter who shows up!

Plus: Help kids of multiple ages discover how to work together as a team, and give young children the extra attention they crave while helping older children feel special as they help younger children learn.

The All-in-One Sunday School Series:
When You Have Kids of All Ages in One Classroom (for ages 4-12)
Lois Keffer

Formerly the Sunday School Specials Series, this revised, updated, and packed series includes original and creative programs designed for ministries with mixed-age classes of children ages 4 through 12! With 13 lessons in each book, this series can last an entire year. Everything's here—including special programming for the seasons and holidays. This series will work in any ministry, but it's especially great for smaller churches that combine classes every Sunday. Also good for large churches that combine ages during summer and for any other multi-age class setting.

▶ VOL. 1 (Fall) • 978-0-7644-4944-4   Only **$24.99** each!